Turning the Tide

Turning the Tide

The Top Ten Principles of
a Success Mindset

Rebekah Harkness

BIONIC
Press
www.bionicpressbooks.com

Cover design by Rebekah Harkness

Published by BIONIC Press
Salt Lake City, UT 84088

Manufactured in the United States of America
ISBN: 978-0-9892448-1-7

To all the dreamers who hear the subtle voice within assuring them of the happiness, peace, and success that patiently awaits

Contents

Introduction

Success is an inside job. There is just no other way around it. We reap what we sow on every level right down to the invisible, including our thoughts, our attitudes, and our mindset. We live in a perfect ever-expanding universe that was meticulously architected to foster our success. Our world is a perfect assortment of control and chaos that is governed by specific universal laws.

The secret to success is to understand how to use these universal laws to your advantage and to be aware of how your thoughts, feelings, and actions create your reality. You master the invisible, and as a result, you master your life.

This book is a compilation of what I believe to be the top ten principles of a success mindset. Although I am simply scratching the surface on a variety of topics, these ideas can open your mind to the power that you hold within yourself. Upon reading this book, you will realize that the infinite laws of the universe are at your disposal and patiently waiting your command.

The time is now to change your life and live the life you have always imagined. The only reason why you aren't living the life of your dreams now is because you haven't tapped into the unlimited source of power within yourself, so get reading.

You alone have created your reality simply through your thoughts. This might be a little hard to swallow at first, but the fact is, you are a direct reflection of your past thoughts. No exception. So let me ask you, what do you think about your current life situation? When you take a look at yourself and take a look at your life, how do you feel? Are you content, sad, frustrated, disappointed, or happy? Are you living the life of your dreams? If you are not, I am here to provide you with some insight that can be applied to improve your life. My goal is to help you get to where you are trying to go by working from the inside out and offering you a better understanding of what role you are playing in the layout of your life.

My hope and joyous expectation is that you will find the writings of this book mind-opening. My intention is to help stretch your level of awareness and consciousness so you will reach for new heights of peace and accomplishment, as did I, when I gained and applied this priceless information. I feel happy and at peace knowing this will be the beginning of a new and improved reality for you. Enjoy the ride.

1

The Power of Your Thoughts

We are nothing more than the sum of our thoughts. We create our reality from the inside out. I am sure that at some point in your life you were introduced to the idea of positive thinking, but do you fully understand the power of your thoughts? Perhaps you bought into the importance of being an optimist versus a pessimist, but do you understand the reason behind it? As you gain a better understanding of yourself and the world around you, you will come to understand why your life and reality is the way that it is.

James Allen, like many of the enlightened individuals of the past and present, likens the mind to a garden. You have the choice and control to either cultivate your garden purposefully by your thoughts or you can allow it to run wild and be subject and determined by everything else but yourself. Regardless of which method you choose, your reality will reflect the essence of your mental garden.

As you go through life, you can choose to allow others to plant seeds in your garden and take no responsibility for it or you can be the creative master that you are and cultivate a beautiful garden as you consciously control your thoughts and create your destiny. Every thought produces a result in your physical reality. We literally reap what we sow on many levels. Your outer world of experience is shaped by your inner world of thought.

We live in a universe of cause and effect. Everything in the universe is connected with this never-ending chain of reaction. A cause creates an effect, then that effect becomes a cause of something else. Your thoughts are the ultimate cause in your life.

Your thoughts create your beliefs. Your beliefs drive your habits, and your habits determine your reality. Let me illustrate this point with a few simple examples. Let's say that as a child you were teased because you were considered overweight in the eyes of others and labeled as fat. At first, you didn't know what to think so you ignored the teasing, but eventually, it wore on you and you started to question whether you should consider yourself to be fat or not. And ever so slowly, their thoughts about you being fat became your thoughts and you accepted it as truth and formulated the belief that you were fat.

Beliefs are simply thoughts that have been repeated over and over until they become a formulated truth in your mind. Going back to the example above, because you have formulated the belief that you are fat, you begin to feel fat. Your emotions and feelings are going to reflect your beliefs and dependent upon your beliefs about what it means to be fat. You might feel ashamed, embarrassed, feel like a failure or not good enough, sad worthless, or perhaps feel nothing. If you held the belief that it was cool to be fat, then you would feel happy and excited.

At this point, your thoughts, beliefs, and feelings drive your actions. Let's assume that because you have come to the conclusion that you are fat, you feel ashamed and embarrassed. Because you feel ashamed and embarrassed you withdraw socially and isolate yourself, your self-esteem suffers, and you feel worthless. Because you have assigned this fat identity to yourself, your subconscious mind affirms the belief that you are fat by compelling you to do things you think fat people should do.

Your subconscious mind operates on compulsion and is constantly directed by your conscious mind. Rational and bias do not exist in your subconscious mind. It simply takes commands from you through your thoughts and uses compulsion to play them out. If you hold the belief that you are fat, your subconscious mind will make that your reality. Unfortunately, with the aid of the Law of Attraction, a snowball effect of self-defeating thoughts, feelings, and actions are activated. As years go by, you live the life of your self-defined image of a fat person until you make the decision to change your thoughts and belief.

Here is another example to illustrate the chain reaction initiated by your thoughts. Let's say you hold the belief that you speak well in front of people. Because you hold this belief about yourself, when asked to present information in front of a group, you would remain calm, collected, and confident. Your actions would reflect your confidence and, as a result, you would do well.

On the other hand, if you hold the belief that you are horrible speaking in front of groups and were asked to present information, you would immediately become anxious and feel inadequate. As a result, you would manifest your internal belief and do poorly. It then becomes a self-fulfilling prophecy. Whatever you believe will manifest in your reality.

Because beliefs are so powerful in shaping the reality of your life, it is extremely important that you don't compare yourself to others. When you compare yourself to others, you cultivate a breeding ground for self-defeating beliefs. As a result, it is very easy to form negative beliefs about yourself in the process. Avoid it like the plague. Keep your attention on yourself and rejoice in the success of others trusting that you will soon reach your own level of success through the conscious effort of controlling your thoughts. You too can live the life you have always imagined.

The important thing to understand here is that you create your own mindset through your thoughts and beliefs, and then ultimately, your mindset creates you. Not only does it create you on a mental and spiritual level, it also creates you on a physical level as well. Your mind is the master of your body. Like everything else, disease and health are determined by thought. Negative thoughts facilitate an environment that welcomes disease. Fear, anxiety, depression, and resentment can potentially destroy your immune system and health as quickly as infectious bacteria or a virus. On the other hand, thoughts of health and well-being create health and well-being. Your body responds to your thoughts and strengthens its defenses while functioning at an optimum level.

In order to change your results, it is necessary to analyze and think about what your thoughts and mindset revolve around. What results are you currently getting? Your results are a direct reflection of your thoughts. So what have you been thinking about? What core beliefs are holding you back from your dreams? Perhaps you don't think you are good enough, worthy enough, smart enough, or savvy enough. Perhaps you are afraid to fail, afraid to succeed, or afraid to be happy. If you feel fear, it is being created by a negative self-belief in your mind. Find it and replace it with a better belief that serves you. Remember, your beliefs are simply thoughts that have been repeated over and over. In order to replace an old belief, it is necessary to repeat the new thought until over time it becomes a belief. This is where the power of affirmations comes into play.

Affirmations are statements that describe a goal or state of being as already achieved. As a form of auto-suggestion, you can use affirmations to create new and improved beliefs. Effective affirmations always start with the words "I am" and are stated in the positive, meaning, you would want to say, "I am happy driving my Mercedes -Benz" versus "I am not happy with my current car." The reason for this is because your subconscious mind thinks in pictures so using the phrase "I am not happy with my current car" causes your subconscious mind to focus on the picture of your current car and thereby maintains your current reality, so always state your affirmations in the positive.

Here is a good example of an affirmation: *I am happily driving my new 2008 black Mercedes-Benz with chrome rims down the street by my house*. It is important to be as specific as you can so that it will spark your mind to form a picture and attach positive feelings to it. You need to be able to see yourself there, feel it, hear it, and perhaps even smell it. Use your five senses to bring it to life. Again, the idea is to visualize your affirmation as you say it by forming a mental image of it in your mind.

What you need to understand is that your subconscious mind works with what you hold in your conscious mind. If you never bring in the idea or picture of you owning a Mercedes-Benz into your consciousness, then your subconscious has nothing to work with and you will never get it. I would like to encourage you to formulate some affirmations based on your goals and aspirations and repeat them to yourself in the morning and at night while visualizing them as you read them. You will be amazed at the results.

In conclusion, take control of your life by taking control of your thoughts. You create yourself and your life from the inside out. In order to successfully change your life, you must change your thoughts. If you find yourself thinking negative self-defeating thoughts, recognize it and immediately change the thought. This will take much effort at first because you have to slowly change your habitual thinking patterns that have nestled themselves in your subconscious and operating mechanisms, but it will get easier as you begin to build new habits. Change your life, literally one thought at a time.

2

Act from the Outcome

Dreams aren't realized by thinking alone. In the very popular movie and book, "The Secret", much attention is placed on our thoughts and how our thoughts relate to the Law of Attraction, but thinking alone will not magically create the life of your dreams. You must act on your thoughts. As I illustrated in the previous chapter, your thoughts are where it all begins. The important thing to understand is your actions are where it all ends.

If your thoughts aren't in alignment with your goals and dreams, your actions won't be either. Remember, your thoughts determine your feelings, behaviors, and habits. Your habits are fueled and formed by your persistent ways of thinking. On the road to success, it is critical to understand the correlation between your thoughts, feelings, and behaviors. They are all interrelated and connected to each other, so it is important to take control of your thoughts in order to create the feelings and habits that will help you get to your desired outcome.

Wishful thinking alone isn't going to get you that beach house that you constantly envision or that beautiful sports car that you so badly want to drive. In order to get what you want, you need to act on it and work towards the outcome that you want. Incorporating the principles of the Law of Attraction, you need to use your thoughts to catapult you on your way to feeling and acting from your desired outcome. Let me illustrate what this looks like and illuminate the differences between acting from the outcome versus acting toward your desired outcome.

If you were to act towards the outcome, you are acting on thoughts starting with "I want". An example would be, "I want to have a beautiful house right on the beach" or "I want to lose 10 pounds." On the contrary, when you are acting from the outcome, you are operating on thoughts that start with "I am". An example would be, "I am enjoying my new house right on the beach" or "I am 135 lbs and loving it!"

The Law of Attraction reacts very differently to these two sets of thoughts. When you have thoughts of "I want…", you are re-enforcing the lack in your life because when you say you want something, it sends a message to the universe that you don't have it yet, so keep it that way. When you have thoughts of "I am", the Law of

Attraction has no other choice but to bring into your life the essence of that vibration. When you are thinking, feeling, and acting from the outcome, the universe assists you in materializing your goals and dreams. When you are thinking, feeling, and acting towards the outcome, you are keeping yourself in a vibrational holding pattern that will bring you only more of the same as the majority of your focus is on your current situation and circumstances.

Here is an example to illustrate the power of acting from your desired outcome. Let's assume that you want to lose 15 lbs and become physically fit. If you were acting from the outcome, you would create a simple affirmation that you would say to yourself every day in the morning and at night that starts with the words, "I am". For example, "I am enjoying my lean fit body, my ability to feel comfortable in my clothes, and my confident demeanor."

In your effort to act from the outcome, you would start asking yourself questions like, "If I were a lean fit healthy person, what would I do on a daily basis? What would I eat? How much sleep should I get?" You would mindstorm possible answers. Perhaps you would come to the conclusion that lean fit healthy people exercise on a daily basis, eat healthy, drink plenty of water, and get enough sleep. So as you act from the outcome, you incorporate these things into your life and begin to "play the role" of a lean healthy person. You start working out at the gym 3-4 times a week, you make efforts to eat healthier, and drink plenty of water. You even begin to think deeply before you make daily decisions when it comes to eating and health. Perhaps, you might ask yourself before you decide to drive to McDonald's, "Would a healthy fit person be driving to McDonald's for dinner?" Well, I think it is safe to say that would be a no. The power behind this concept is that as you act from your desired outcome as if you are already there, by default, you eventually arrive.

James Arthur Ray, a leader and popular speaker, is very much a believer in action as well as thought. In his most recent book, *Harmonic Wealth*, James Arthur Ray talks about the importance of what he likes to call "Going 3-for-3". James points out the importance that your thoughts, feelings, and actions need to be in harmony with your desired outcome. Without any one of those three components, you won't accomplish your goal. In order to keep your thoughts, feelings, and actions in alignment with your desired outcome, it is necessary to be constantly aware of what you are doing with your mind. Because thoughts are the ultimate cause behind your feelings, actions, and everything else in your life, your focus should be in controlling and being aware of your thoughts. If your thoughts are in alignment with your goal, you are setting the stage for appropriate feelings and actions to follow.

For example, let's say you have a goal of getting a Master's Degree in Business Administration. You are excited so you begin visualizing and thinking about having that degree. You even create an affirmation related to this goal that you read every morning before you go to work. Well, unless you begin to take action as well, you aren't going to get very far. Perhaps, you could begin looking at admission requirements, start studying for the GRE, thinking about how you would pay for it, etc. Without the action piece, you just won't ever get there.

Let me give you a less obvious example. Let's say you have a goal or desired outcome to become debt-free within the next year. Well, based on what you know about the principles of the Law of Attraction, you keep your attention off of your debt (because that is what you don't want), and you begin to form positive thoughts related to money. As a result of your efforts, you are doing a good job keeping your thoughts in alignment with your goal of being debt free, but unfortunately, every time you open your Visa bill you feel anxiety about your debt and worry about how you are going to ever get out of it. Because your feelings are not in alignment with your desired outcome, your anxiety paralyzes you and limits any actions you might take to try to find a solution or relief from your debt. See how this works? Even though this is a very simple and powerful concept, it appears a lot easier than it really is. It takes work and a lot of effort to be constantly aware of the direction of your thoughts, feelings, and actions, but it can be done. I guarantee if you pay attention to your thoughts, feelings, and actions while keeping your goal or desired outcome in mind, your dreams will become a reality and the universe will be at your command.

An important aspect of acting from the outcome includes making decisions based on where you are going, not where you have been. Remember, your current level of results or in other words, your life, is nothing more than the residual outcome of your past thoughts, feelings, and actions. Your body, your health, your house, your bank account, you car, your marriage or relationship, your job, your happiness, or lack thereof, is nothing more than a reflection of who you are.

The results in your life, in every area, are simply a biofeedback mechanism to what you have been doing with your thoughts, feelings, and actions. Your results are a mirror of who you are at this moment, so think about this for a minute and go stand in front of a mirror. What do you see? Remember mirrors don't judge, they don't say whether something is good or bad, nor is their perspective skewed in any way. Mirrors simply reflect back the image of what's put forth. See where I am going with this? Think about all aspects of your life including your health, your house, your marriage or relationship, your job, your bank account, etc. and think about the fact that your results are a direct reflection of who you are right now.

Now one thing I want you to understand very clearly is that what you are looking at in the mirror has nothing to do with your potential and what you are capable of becoming, unless of course you accept what you see and continue to make decisions based on those results and based on where you have been. You will simply create more of the same. Again, if you want different results in all areas of your life, then make decisions based on where you are going, not where you have been.

As human beings, we are habitual creatures. We like routine. Based on our personality and past experiences, some like it more than others, but regardless, routine is very much a part of all of our lives. There is safety in routine, and there is also control. As a result, change can be very challenging for us because we get comfortable and accustomed to our environment and how things are. As you make an effort to make decisions based on where you are going and not where you have been, it is important to be aware of that voice inside your head and what you say when you talk to yourself.

Now, when I reference the voice inside your head, I want to be perfectly clear that I am not talking about your intuition. Intuition is more feeling-based. I am specifically talking about when you talk to yourself inside your head. For example, let's say that you have been thinking about going back to school because you have always wanted to be a nurse, but every time you consider it that voice inside your head comes up with 20 different reasons why you can't do it. Maybe the voice inside your head tells you that you can't afford it, there is no way that you would be able to find a babysitter for the kids, you aren't smart enough, you might fail or you might not finish. As a result, you put off going to school.

Here is another example, let's say there is a leadership position open at work, and you really want the job, but again, that voice inside your head begins to tell you all the reasons why you can't do it or you shouldn't do it. Maybe it says you aren't qualified, you don't have the competencies they are looking for, you hate getting rejected, or perhaps the voice simply tells you, you just aren't good enough. Again, as a result, you succumb to that voice in your head and don't apply for the position.

Now I want you to do yourself a favor and challenge that voice inside your head. Right now with me, I want you to think back to the last conversation you had with yourself in regards to a decision you were making, and I want you to ask yourself what was the underlying emotion or feeling behind the voice inside your head? Was it fear, rejection, anxiety, self-doubt, pessimism, or worry? Or was it encouragement, excitement, optimism, joy, or confidence?

Once you take a step back and analyze the impact of the voice inside your head, you will notice a theme or a pattern regardless of the situation. If you have a lot of fear or anxiety in reaction to a specific situation, you are probably going to react in a similar way in another situation because that voice inside your head is going to operate on the same emotions and either hold you back from your goals and dreams or help get you there. You have been the one that has programmed this voice inside your head by your habitual thought patterns of the past, so if you want to change the operating emotions behind your inner voice, you must change your thoughts and also challenge what the voice is trying to tell you so that you can make better decisions.

For instance, let's go back to the example about the individual wanting to go back to school and become a nurse. Their internal voice questioned whether they could afford it financially, so let's talk about how they could challenge that idea. To challenge it, they could ask themselves what possibilities are out there for individuals wanting to go back to school that don't have the money. They could then do research and find there are many government funding programs and scholarships available. What about the babysitting problem? Well, they could first start by asking family members, neighbors, and friends to see if they would be willing to help out.

The point is this: First, figure out what emotions or feelings are driving your internal voice and then raise your personal awareness. If negative emotions are driving that voice inside your head, like fear, anxiety, self-doubt, or pessimism, they are holding you back from your goals. Step back and challenge the voice. Think about what is determining the underlying emotional tone and decide if you want them guiding your life. Do you want your life guided and determined by fear, anxiety or self-doubt or do you want it guided by excitement, encouragement, optimism, joy, and confidence?

Pay attention to your thoughts, feelings, and actions, and work hard to keep them all in alignment with your goals and dreams. As you act from the outcome and keep your desired result in the forefront of your mind, it will be easier to make decisions based on where you are going and not where you have been. Challenge the voice inside your head and know that in order to change your results, you have to change your reaction to that voice.

3

Taking Responsibility

If there was one question that had the power to change your life, this question could be the one. Do you take 100% responsibility for your life? Now, before answering, I really want you to think about this for a minute. When I say 100%, I really do mean 100%, so think about it.

If you are like most people, you are probably thinking about the many reasons why you shouldn't have to take 100% responsibility for your life. You could probably give me a long list of reasons why things didn't work out perfectly for you. Perhaps, you were born into the wrong family, your family was poor and didn't foster opportunity for you, you were discriminated against for whatever reason, you had lousy parents, no support, were surrounded by the wrong group of friends, or maybe you were teased and scapegoated on countless occasions. I know, I know. You could go on and on, but let me stop you right there and introduce some ideas that might change your thinking a bit.

The problem with excuses is that they focus your attention on lack and hold you in a pattern of stagnation. By not taking responsibility for yourself in everything you do, you are placing your power on external circumstance and forfeiting the unlimited power you hold within yourself. You are holding your fate and your success in the hands of everyone around you as you sit and watch everything unfold. You might as well make yourself comfortable and grab some popcorn and a drink.

By not taking complete responsibility for your life and your results, you are passing the baton to everyone else and expecting them to follow through for you. Do you honestly want your fate to be in their hands?

The beauty about life is that regardless of your circumstances growing up and regardless of your circumstances now, you have all the capability and power you will ever need to make your dreams come true and create the life you want. The answers to the many questions in your heart can't be answered externally, but rather, the answers already exist in you. You have all the power you will ever need.

Unfortunately, as we grow up and mature in this world, we are programmed to believe in fear, limitation, and disappointment. It seems like our fear of failure gets bigger and bigger as the years go by. We come into this world completely fearless. We don't even know what fear is, but then we are introduced to fear by our family and friends. We are told what our perceived limitations are, what we can't do based on what other people have done, and why we shouldn't dream big because there only lies disappointment ahead. Not only are we told what we can't do, but the people around us provide many perceived reasons why what they are telling us is true. Mind you, their point of reference is their own experience so if it was something that they couldn't do, then automatically they are going to transfer their limiting perceptions on you and tell you that you can't do it either. It is important to not let their failures creep into your reality. Don't accept their limited thinking.

As I look back into my childhood, it is interesting to think about the many things that I was told that I couldn't do, which by the way I did do. Thankfully as a child, when someone told me that I couldn't do something, it simply pushed me that much harder. I remember thinking, "Huh? Because I am a girl I can't do what?!?"

It is easy to buy into all the lies, and it seems like by the time we are adults we wear our excuses like badges of honor and have our playback button ready if anyone asks us why we didn't follow and accomplish our dreams. I bet you can think of your ready-to-playback answers already on standby just in case someone asks you about it.

The point is this: Let the excuses go and take 100% responsibility for your life. It's time. Let go of all the pain, the hurt, the resentment, the missed opportunities, the struggles, and the contempt. Every human being on this planet, including yourself, at every given moment is doing the best they can with the skills, knowledge, and understanding that they have available to them at that point in time. No more no less. Your parents did the best they could with the skills, knowledge, and understanding that they had while raising you. Maybe in all reality they sucked. Perhaps maybe you were even neglected or abused. If so, I am sorry. The good news is that you have the will to heal and the power to heal. No damage is permanent unless you allow it to be. Make the decision to heal and take 100% responsibility for your life.

If you are holding on to a grudge or if you are holding onto some pain caused by someone in your past, let it go. Again, have the perspective that they did the best they could with the skills, knowledge, and understanding that they had at the time. Their reaction was a complete reflection of their personal level of understanding and emotional maturity. I am sure that you can think of times when you yourself perhaps didn't make the best decision and hurt someone else. Again, I can't say this enough... you did the best you could. Forgive yourself, learn from it, and let it go. You can't afford to have part of your energy stuck in the past. If you want to move forward toward your goals and dreams, you are going to need your full attention and energy in the present moment, so let it all go. You are holding yourself hostage by playing those thoughts and feelings over and over in your mind and heart. Focus your attention on where you are going, not where you have been, and prepare yourself to take 100% responsibility and change your outcomes.

Your life is a series of outcomes that weave in and out to create the fabric of your experience. In Jack Canfield's most recent book, *The Success Principles*, he introduces an easy-to-understand formula that illustrates how outcomes are created and how you can change the outcomes in your life. This formula also illustrates the importance and necessity of taking 100% responsibility for your life.

The formula is this:

$$E + R = O$$
Event + Response = Outcome

The basic premise of this formula is that every outcome in your life, whether it be a success or failure, is the result of a life event and your response to that event. In other words, your response to any event in your life is a contributing factor to the outcome.

Now, if you aren't getting the outcomes that you want in your life, there are only two conclusions that you can make. Either you can take the approach of blaming the event for your lousy outcome and taking zero responsibility for it or you can change your response to the event, and as a result, change the outcome.

You obviously can't change an event that occurs in your life, so the only choice you have in affecting the outcome is by controlling your response. Let me give you an example to illustrate the power behind this simple formula. Imagine that you own a small restaurant, and for the last six months as part of your marketing campaign, you have been mailing out flyers to consumers in your surrounding area. Unfortunately, you haven't seen good results. Traffic is slow, and you aren't making much profit, so it is time to evaluate what your next step should be.

Using the formula as our guide, let's take a look at different ways this situation could be handled. One approach could include blaming the poor economy, high gas prices, or high unemployment rate as potential reasons why people aren't coming to your restaurant, and you keep doing what you are doing. Another approach could include taking responsibility for the results and making the decision to do something different. You could discontinue using the mailing service and try a different marketing approach.

I want you to notice that placing blame on something isn't going to change your outcome. In this example, blame was placed and nothing was done differently. You can't expect different results if you are going to continue to do the exact same thing. You will continue to get what you have always got. By taking a different approach and focusing on your response, you are giving yourself the opportunity to do something different. In the second approach, a different course of action was chosen, and a different outcome was created. It is very important that you understand this concept because this principle alone has the power to change your life immediately.

Take 100% responsibility for your results. If you do, you are giving yourself the opportunity to change your outcomes. Isn't that the ultimate goal here? You are reading this book because that is exactly what you are interested in - changing your outcomes in order to get to where you are trying to go.

So, go for it. The quicker you take complete responsibility for your life, the quicker you will find the motivation to change it. There is so much power in taking 100% responsibility for your life. Speaking from personal experience, once I adopted this principle, I had a complete paradigm shift in the way I looked at my life. I no longer had any excuses nor did I need them. I was in control. I was in the driver's seat, and all I cared about was where I was going and how I was going to get there. All my energy was focused in the present. Immediately, I was energized and felt lighter than I had my entire life. I would like to encourage you to do the same. Metaphorically speaking, pack your bags, leave them at the door, and get to work.

4

Be in the Present

I remember sitting in 10th grade English class. My teacher was leaning up against her desk addressing the class. She had a slight touch of irritation in her voice as she was reprimanding the entire class for not being on task. The reason for the reprimand I don't know, but one sentence that she said has stuck with me for years. She said simply,"Be where you are."

At first, I remember thinking how silly that sounded, and now years later, I have begun to unravel the enormity of importance behind that simple, yet profound sentence. I used to wonder if she even knew the power behind that sentence. The fact remains, your point of power is completely in your present.

Being in the present moment was something I

learned over time. Growing up, I was an anxiety-ridden individual who walked around on eggshells hoping to stay on the so-called "straight and narrow". Looking back, almost everything I did was in an effort to minimize the potential of feeling anxious. I got straight A's, stayed out of trouble, and tried to be who I was expected to be. My being was always consumed with anxiety and fear, which were byproducts of my environment and lack of self-worth. Don't get me wrong, I wasn't ridden with panic or anxiety attacks, but I was definitely imprisoned by it.

One benefit was that I made good decisions, which helped push me to the front of the class so to speak, but the negative habitual thought pattern associated with this type of mindset was very detrimental. I had a lot of work to do to find peace and well-being, so I took it one step at a time, or better stated, one thought at a time.

The fact is your point of power is in your present. It isn't in your past, and it isn't in your future. Your future begins in the here and now. Energy flows where attention goes. If your attention is constantly in the past, not only is the moment passing you by, but your focus is on your past results. If you focus on your past results, you will continue to get what you have always got. Your results will not change. This happens for a couple of reasons. One reason is because your point of attraction stays the same. If you are mentally stuck in the past, you have to be operating the same thought processes, which in turn, creates and maintains your point of attraction.

Here is an example to illustrate what this looks like. People who are in relationships ruled by domestic violence often go from one abusive relationship to the next. As horrible and painful as the previous relationship was, they often find themselves in a similar hell during their next relationship. An outsider might wonder how that could happen. Why would they put themselves in that position again? Because our thoughts create our point of attraction and reality, and our thoughts are the ultimate cause in our lives. If our thoughts remain stuck in the past and we make no effort to change them, we will continue to repeat the same scenario until we learn our lesson and change our thoughts. People who go from one abusive relationship to the next are lost in their thoughts of poor self-worth and low self-esteem. Until they change their thoughts, the essence of their reality won't change.

Another reason the results won't change is that if part of your energy is focused on the past, you only have a limited amount of energy free to improve and change your current reality. This truth is evident when an individual is caught up in resentment, revenge, or bitterness. When you allow yourself to feel any of these emotions, you are holding yourself captive and limiting your ability to move forward. You are allowing an event of the past to continue to poison and affect present and future. Do you honestly want to give someone that much power over you?

Forgiveness is important here. When you forgive somebody, it isn't for them, but for you. To forgive someone who has wronged you is one of the best things that you can do for yourself. Whether it be your parents, a friend, a relative, or even a complete stranger that has wronged you in some way, it is time to let the pain go. One thing to understand is that every single one of us does the best we can with the knowledge and emotional maturity we have available at that moment. Maybe in all reality your parents were inadequate, but the fact is they did the best they could with what they had to work with. Let it go. Forgive them for their shortcomings and love them for who they are. Don't let resentment, bitterness, or vengeful thinking keep you locked in the past. The past is over. What you have now is this very moment, so what are you going to do with it? You can either use it to brood about things that you can't change or use it to get to where you want to go.

Another emotion that originates out of the past is guilt. Guilt is a mechanism that holds you hostage in the past. Think about it. Things that you feel guilty for happened in the past. It is impossible to feel guilty about something in the present. It doesn't work. People don't realize that forgiveness for yourself is just as important as forgiving someone else. We do the best we can with the skills and emotional maturity that we have at our disposal at any given moment. We are here to learn and grow, and you can't grow without making mistakes along the way. Learn from them and forgive yourself. If you find yourself feeling guilty, it would be a good idea to self-reflect and look at why you think it is necessary to feel guilty. How does your guilt serve you? Is it your way of punishing yourself for your wrong-doing? It is necessary to locate the beliefs you hold about yourself that facilitate guilt and change those beliefs. Remember, the only one affected by your guilt is you. You are making the choice to feel guilty and it only exists in your mind. Your thoughts created it. Why do that to yourself? The bottom line is that guilt is absolutely useless and detrimental. It will hold you hostage in the past and steal your dreams minute by minute.

It is important to keep in mind that you can't change the past. What is done is done. You can change your future by changing your thoughts in the present. Your point of power is in the here and now. This moment. If you think about it, your future is simply a series of present moments strung together moment by moment. If you improve the present moment, by default, you are improving your future. Don't waste your time in the past focusing on things that you can't change, while moments you have control over simply pass you by.

Victims live in the past. The majority of their thoughts are focused on times when they were wronged in some way. If you are stuck in a victim mindset, you will consistently live in the past. Your thoughts will revolve around times in your life when you endured an injustice of some kind and allowed yourself to feel powerless. Victim mindsets are completely debilitating. You carry a moment of powerlessness on for days and days and even years. You are held hostage by your thoughts, and you refuse to take responsibility for your life. How can you take responsibility for your life if you are stuck in bitterness, pity, powerlessness, and anger? As a result of your victim mindset, you have convinced yourself that your current life situation is simply the result of other people's actions, bad luck, or a combination of the two. Because you take little responsibility for your life, you have little incentive to change anything, so…you don't. Why would you change if you carry the belief that your circumstances are caused by others?

In order to avoid a victim mindset, it is important to take responsibility for your life. Realize that your current life situation is a direct reflection of you, your thoughts, and your choices. Take responsibility and change your life. Let go of your past, figure out what you want in life, and direct all of your attention on the present moment so that you can work moment by moment to build your future.

As you work in the present to build your future, there is another emotion that you should be aware of. A negative emotion of the future is anxiety and worry. When you are anxious, you aren't anxious about things that happened in the past, but you are anxious about potential things to come. You worry about things or events that don't even exist yet or won't ever exist.

Anxiety is a very interesting emotion to me. Like I previously mentioned, I used to be the queen of anxiety. I was anxious and fearful of many things, more specifically, many outcomes. I had successfully programmed my mind to almost always expect an awful outcome, if not the worse possible outcome. As a result, I was constantly fighting against this programming. Life was a drag, and it slowly wore on me. Everything came at such a high cost emotionally because I was so anxiety-ridden. Eventually, I figured out the origin of this anxious programming, and I changed my thought habits. Every time I would begin to feel anxious about something I would ask myself, "What is the worst thing that could happen?" As soon as I answered that question in each situation, I would get control of my thoughts and focus my attention on a positive outcome. I would visualize the outcome I wanted and bring myself back in the present. At first, it was amazing to me how powerful being in the present really was. What a simple concept.

Anxiety freezes you in your tracks. It makes an attempt to paralyze you in fear using images and outcomes that are not real. If there is anything to be fearful of, it is fear and anxiety itself. Negative thinking and detrimental thought patterns destroy your life from the inside out because you get what you think about whether you want it or not.

In summary, be in the present. Live moment by moment as you build the foundation of your future. If you are feeling guilty, recognize that you are stuck in the past and you are holding yourself hostage to your past results. If your focus is on your past, you will continue to get what you have always got.

If you feel yourself weighed down with bitterness, resentment, or revenge, forgiveness is necessary. Don't let a past event continue to affect your present reality and shape your future. That would be equivalent to you relinquishing every ounce of your power. The past is over. Don't relive it over and over in your mind. Let it go.

If you find yourself ridden with anxiety and worry, ask yourself,"What is the worst thing that could happen?" Operate with a joyous expectancy of the best and visualize a positive outcome. Change your thinking habits one thought at a time. Be in the present, for the present is all we have.

5

Using the 7 Super Laws of the Universe

Ever since I was a teenager and began to figure out what I wanted in life, I always wondered what the difference was between someone who had money, success, and prosperity versus someone who did not. Looking back, I distinctly remember being young, walking by a gentleman who appeared downtrodden and homeless, and wondering what differentiated him and me. Questions would flood my mind like - How did he get to that point in his life? Why would he let that happen? Was it out of his control? If so, how am I immune from that happening to me? Did he choose that life? What keeps him there in that state of being? How can such poverty exist in such an abundant world? Being surrounded in a world of abundance and opportunity, why could he not get his hands on some of it?

As I grew older, I continued to be curious and fascinated with this dichotomy of scarcity and abundance. It slowly became a question consistently on my mind. Regardless of hard work, education, or privilege, why do some people make it big and others do not? I had a feeling that there was something else going on, and I was bound and determined to figure it out. Not until after I gained an understanding of the universal Super Laws and the power of our thoughts did I realize what really separated a successful individual and someone who just can't quite get there.

The bottom line is if you want to catapult yourself on the pathway to success and abundance, it is necessary to understand these universal laws and apply them to your life. After reading this chapter, I encourage you to use your newly acquired awareness to put yourself in better alignment with these laws. Think about them and look for evidence of these laws in your life as well as those around you. I guarantee you will find overwhelming evidence of the impact these laws play in shaping the reality of your life. You will then choose to apply the principles of these laws consciously in your life. As you apply these principles, you will see improved results in your life. Remember, these laws are scientific and have stood the test of time.

We live in a universe of order perfectly balanced by a mixture of chaos and control. These laws exist whether you pay attention to them or not, so you might as well use them to your advantage. The more understanding you have of yourself and the world around you, the more you can anticipate and understand your circumstances, and as a result, improve your life.

In order to be successful, it is absolutely necessary to understand and utilize the Super Laws of the universe. All successful individuals use these laws to succeed whether they are aware of it or not. As you understand and apply the principles associated with these laws of the universe, you are choosing success and setting up the universe to work for you rather than against you. Again, regardless of the situation, whenever you succeed it is because you are using the principles associated with these laws. No exception.

There are 7 Super Laws that govern everything in the universe and operate under the major premise that everything is energy, including you, the car you drive, your green-tea latte, as well as your smelly socks. As mentioned previously, if you apply the basic principles associated with each of these laws, you will experience success consistently throughout your life. The 7 Super Laws are as follows:

Law of Vibration
Law of Relativity
Law of Rhythm
Law of Polarity
Law of Perpetual Transmutation of Energy

Law of Cause and Effect

Law of Gender

Law of Vibration

The Law of Vibration states that everything in the universe is in a constant state of vibration. Everything is energy vibrating at different frequencies. What differentiates a rock from a table is simply the frequency of their vibrations. Objects in physical form have lower frequencies as compared to thoughts. Thoughts are a form of energy that vibrate at the highest frequency. Because of their high frequency, thoughts can penetrate solids, time and space.

Many people use the word "vibe" without really putting much thought into it when describing a person or the atmosphere in a room. For example, someone might say, "She seemed like a really ornery person, and I didn't like her vibe." Without even realizing it, they are recognizing the fact that they felt her vibrations. Again, everything is energy.

The Law of Vibration gave birth to the Law of Attraction, which states that like attracts like and dissimilar frequencies repel. This is why our thoughts are so incredibly important. We get what we think about whether we want it or not. If we think positively and think about what we want, that is exactly what we get. On the same token, if we think negatively and think about what we don't want, that is exactly what we get.

Law of Relativity

Einstein's Theory of Relativity states that everything in the physical realm exists because of its relationship to something else. I like to call this law, the Law of Comparison. Things exist without meaning until we compare it to something else and assign meaning. For example, cold only exists when compared to hot. If we didn't have hot as a point of reference, we wouldn't recognize cold. We can only define what cold is by using what we know about hot.

The reason this law is important to create success is that it is very easy to create and maintain self-defeating comparisons in your mind that affect the way you think, feel, and act. For example, let's say you make the conclusion that you are poor. In order to make that conclusion you use a point of reference to compare yourself and based on your point of reference, you can either feel poor or feel abundant.

For example, if your point of reference is the income of a famous celebrity, you could feel poor even though you make over $100,000 a year. Now comparing your $100,000 a year to the average income for a small family in the United States, you are rolling in the dough. See where I am going with this?

When you compare yourself to other people in any way, you are setting yourself up for self-defeating beliefs.

Remember, you are the one assigning meaning to an otherwise meaningless thought. If you are creating comparisons in your mind and feeling inadequate, insecure, or not good enough, you are holding yourself hostage because those feelings are setting in motion corresponding thoughts, feelings, and actions of lack, self-doubt, and insecurity.

Law of Rhythm

The Law of Rhythm states that energy is like a pendulum. When there is a swing to the right, there must be a swing to the left. Everything is either growing or dying. There is evidence of this law all around us. For example, the sun rises and the sun sets, the moon rises and the moon sets, night and day, and seasons come and go. Highs and lows exist everywhere whether it be in the stock market, our performance, our moods, or in nature. There is a rhythm to everything. As you increase your awareness of this law, your timing and decision making will improve.

This law can also be seen in the performances of athletes. Professional athletes learn to recognize and adapt to this law so that they can maintain peak performance during important events in their career. This idea is incredibly relevant to Olympians that work and train for four years for one small window of opportunity to obtain the gold medal.

Law of Polarity

According to the Law of Polarity, everything in the universe contains within itself an equivalent opposite. From a quantum physics perspective, every electron, which has a negative charge, must have a matching positron, carrying a positive charge. In lay terms, if there is something that seems really awful there has to be something incredible there as well. Every time, no exception. It is scientific law.

Let me give you a personal example, over eight years ago I was involved in an almost fatal accident. It was a paragliding accident in which I collided with another individual mid-air and dropped over 100 ft. My entire pelvis shattered causing internal bleeding and both my ankles suffered open-compound fractures. I was lucky to be alive and had a long road of recovery ahead of me. Similar to Humpty-Dumpty, the doctors had to piece me back together again and placed internal titanium hardware to keep things in place. From a negative perspective, this accident was heartbreaking. Not only did I have a long recovery ahead of me, but I wasn't ever going to have full-functioning ankles, I was told that my mobility and strength would be limited and that I would never be able to run or jump again. Now from a positive perspective, I was alive. I had the chance to walk again and be up-right. I was under the care of some of the best orthopedic surgeons in my area, and I knew that everything was going to be all right.

I used this heartbreaking experience to get me to where I am today and to learn to embrace what it means to be truly appreciative and grateful. I saw my accident as a "start-over" button….on many levels. On the physical level, I didn't have any other choice but to start over because I had to learn how to walk again. On the emotional and mental level, my accident gave me the opportunity to really figure out what I wanted in life, who and what I needed to purge out of my life, and how I was going to get there. I was more focused than I had ever been. I slowly cleansed myself of the chaos and conflict that attracted the accident into my life in the first place and off I went toward my dreams and goals.

I guarantee that you will experience heartbreak, trials, and adversities, and I also guarantee you that within the heartbreak sits an opportunity to learn and grow. Napoleon Hill, the author of Think and Grow rich, made the statement, "Every adversity, every failure and every heartache carries with it the seed of an equivalent or greater benefit."

Make the decision today to find that opportunity or as Napoleon Hill called it, "the seed". Those seeds will not only get you on the path to success and happiness, but you will also find peace, so have fun growing your garden.

Law of Perpetual Transmutation of Energy

This law states that energy is always moving and

changing. Energy never stands still. In essence, change is all there is. There is no such thing as stagnancy. If you ever feel stagnant, it simply means you are going in circles. Motion and change are constant. Even things that appear solid and stable are moving and changing incessantly. This is evident when things are looked at under a microscope where we witness activity happening on the microscopic level.

Because of this constant motion, everything is either growing or dying. This concept can be applied to any circumstance whether it be the stock market, businesses, relationships, your body, flowers, trees, etc. When I mean everything, I mean everything. When it comes to relationships, every relationship in your life is either growing or dying depending on where you are focusing your energy. There might be times when it is necessary to work long hours for a certain period of time, so as a result, your relationship suffers. Eventually, work slows down and you begin to put more of your energy again into the nurturing of your relationship, and so it goes. Things are in constant motion.

If you can learn to accept and embrace the fact that change is constant and that change is all there is, you will quickly adapt to it and eliminate the fear that holds you hostage.

Law of Cause and Effect

This law states that every effect must have a cause, and every cause must have an effect. It is a continuous chain of events. A cause of a specific effect was an effect of something that came before it. In every day terms, "What goes around comes around."

Ultimately, your thoughts are the primary cause in your life. Your thoughts manifest themselves in your reality and create the effects in your life. As you go about your daily life and make decisions, it is important to be aware what you are creating and forming in your mind will manifest physically in your life.

If you are thinking thoughts based in fear, anxiety, worry, or self-doubt, then those thoughts will manifest themselves in your reality. If you are thinking thoughts based in confidence, love, peace, or abundance, then that is exactly what you will get. Again, your thoughts are the ultimate cause in your life. Your reality has nothing to do with your parents, the economy, the opportunities that you didn't get, or any other excuse that can so easily pop into your head. The results in your life are a direct reflection of your thoughts. Quit blaming other people for your life and focus on within.

The Law of Gender

This law states that everything must have an incubation or gestation period. This gestational period is simply the time frame in which energy changes form. For example, the sperm and egg unite to slowly form a baby. The baby is the result of the transmutation of that energy. Another example of this law is the time it takes for a seed to break ground and grow into a beautiful plant or flower.

The key principle to understand is that energy is neither created nor destroyed. The success you want already exists in a different form. All you need to do is transform the energy into what you want. This concept might be a little hard to understand at first, but once you get it, you will immediately feel empowered and hopeful. I know I did.

Because everything has a gestational period and you won't know how long it will take, it is imperative to have faith and believe in the unseen. Going back to planting a seed, you plant the seed with a complete expectation that it will grow. There isn't a doubt in your mind because that is what happens - seeds grow. It is important to use that same level of faith and expectation as you plant seeds of success in your heart and mind. James Arthur Ray tells us to do the following," Rather than waiting until you see it to believe it, begin to believe it until you see it."

You plant the seed with your desire for success. Your thoughts, feelings, and actions then nurture and water the seed. Stay focused and have faith that as you continue to nurture your seed. Eventually you will see physical evidence as your seed "breaks ground and sprouts forth."

6

Visualization

Visualization is defined as the act of creating pictures in your mind. It has been said that if you have been there in the mind, you will go there in the body. The power of visualization has been talked about and documented for decades, but amongst the general public it is an underutilized tool. We often hear about those stories in which professional athletes use visualization to prepare for a sporting event or a once in a lifetime chance to break a record, but the reality is that everyone could benefit from the use of visualization.

Visualization is a tool you can use to accelerate your path to success. As mentioned by Jack Canfield in his book, *Principles of Success*, visualization can accelerate your success in three ways.

1. Visualization activates creativity in your subconscious mind.

2. Visualization focuses your brain by programming its reticular activating system (RAS) to locate available resources in your memory that were already there, but had previously gone unnoticed.

3. Visualization magnetizes and attracts the people and resources that you will need to achieve your target or goal.

It is a known fact that your brain and nervous system can't tell the difference between a vivid visualization and an actual event in real life. Your mind reacts the same way in either circumstance, which by the way is a huge advantage unless of course you never use it.

When you visualize something on a consistent basis and you use your imagination and emotions to bring it to life, certain things start happening. First of all, simply by the act of your visualization and thinking the thoughts surrounding the event or goal, you are giving your subconscious mind a "green light" and sending it the message that you are welcoming this experience into your reality. Remember, everything that manifests physically began as a thought. No exception. You have to think the thought first before it can appear in your reality. Secondly, visualization programs your brain's reticular activating system

(RAS) to start scanning its resources to locate anything that would help you achieve your goal.

Visualization also activates your subconscious mind to create solutions. It literally puts your subconscious mind to work because when you visualize your goals as already complete, it creates a conflict in your subconscious mind between your visualization and your current reality. Your subconscious mind wants to make it right. As a result, it works through you to make your visualization a reality.

The work of your subconscious mind becomes evident as new ideas come to your awareness. You might think of new ideas when you are in the shower, driving, or relaxing on the couch. Not only will new ideas start popping up, but you will also notice a considerable increase in your motivation. You will find new energy to put more effort into achieving the goal. You will become motivated to do new things that perhaps you hadn't thought of before.

Visualization is one of the easiest things you will ever do. All you have to do is close your eyes and let your imagination run wild. You could visualize a beautiful home that you have always wanted. You could visualize yourself cashing a $100,000 check for services that you rendered. You could also visualize yourself being more social when in all reality you are very shy.

Visualization is something you can benefit from greatly if you do it on a daily basis, even in regards to mundane tasks. You could visualize a task that you have to get done today, and while you are visualizing yourself doing it, focus on the end result as well. Picture the task being done efficiently, and you producing the best results possible. One of the lingering benefits of habitually doing this is that it puts you in a success mindset, where you are focusing on and putting forth your energy toward a successful outcome. By visualizing success, failure is a word that doesn't even exist in your mind. All of your attention and focus is on the successful outcome, and as a result, when you physically attempt to accomplish the task, you are much more likely to succeed and do it efficiently.

Personally, I use visualization while I meditate in the morning. This allows me to mentally paint a picture of what I want my day to look like. If I have important meetings or training, I visualize myself interacting comfortably and communicating effectively. If I have specific tasks that need to be done, I visualize myself doing them efficiently and successfully.

While meditating, after I visualize my day, I begin to visualize one of my goals. I visualize it as already completed, and I try to create the experience in my mind so that I am feeling what it would feel like and seeing as many details as possible.

Visualization is also effective because every living thing has an internal built-in goal striving mechanism, which functions most effectively when we provide a well-defined picture or goal. In his book, *Psycho-Cyber-*

netics, Maxwell Maltz explains the objective of this goal striving mechanism and teaches us how to use it effectively.

According to Maltz, the purpose of the built-in goal striving mechanism is to allow every organism the opportunity to achieve its goal, which in its broadest sense is to live. The goal to live for many organisms is to survive individually as well as preserve the species, find food and shelter, overcome enemies and obstacles, and to procreate.

This goal striving mechanism is very evident in animals. For example, a squirrel doesn't have to be taught to gather nuts. It simply does it. Nor does a bird have to take lessons in nest-building or navigation. The bird somehow knows when cold weather is coming and how to get to warmer climate. For animals, the goals are pre-set and all related to survival and preservation.

As humans, our goal to live consists of much more than survival and preservation. Beyond the survival needs, we also have emotional and spiritual needs. As a result, our goal striving mechanism, also known as our success mechanism, has a much broader scope and allows us to problem solve, run a business, invent new products, build a house, and succeed in any activity that we choose to participate in.

The process by which our goal-striving mechanism works is through trial and error. It helps steer us in the right direction by using information and data that has been gathered from previous successes and failures. As data is collected, each success is remembered as well as each failure. Maxwell Maltz further explains that as a baby is learning how to use its muscles, the difficulty in reaching for an object is obvious. The baby has little, if any, stored information to draw upon to assist it in achieving its goal, so its hand zigzags and flops around a bit until eventually it reaches the object. During this process, its goal striving mechanism, or in other words its success mechanism, was gathering information and learning from the failures in order to eventually succeed.

Another example is someone learning how to play baseball and specifically how to catch fly balls. At first, when the ball is in the air, the individual isn't going to have much information to go off of in terms of how the trajectory and speed of the ball affects the distance. Over time, as more attempts are made and the success mechanism gathers more information through experience, namely successes and failures, they eventually become really good at catching fly balls. As a result, they instinctively know where the ball is going to land and where they need to be to catch it.

I would like to encourage you to read Maxwell Maltz' book, *Psycho-Cybernetics*. He goes into detail about how we can use our goal-striving mechanism to the fullest and create the life that we have always wanted. What I would like you to understand at this point is that your goal-striving mechanism needs to have a goal to work on. By using visualization, you are creating that goal and creating a vivid picture for your success mechanism to work with.

As kids, each one of us had big hopes and big dreams. I think it is safe to assume that as you would share your untainted desires and dreams, there were countless adults standing by to squash them. The word "can't" slowly became one of the most prominent thoughts in your head. As a result, it became harder and harder to dream.

There are numerous people in our lives that love to tell us how hard life is, how disappointing life is, and how it is better not to dream because you don't want to be disappointed in the end. Well, it is time for a different mindset. Dream-stealers love company, but don't be tempted to take the seat that they are offering right next to them. When somebody tells you that it can't be done, it is simply a reflection of their inability to realize their potential. By reading this book, you are already on your way.

Dream big and give your unlimited goal-striving success mechanism something to work for. Use visualization to paint the pictures. While visualizing, be as specific as you can. If you want a house on the beach, visualize every last detail. Smell the water and listen to the waves. What color is the paint on the wall? What color are the dishes in your kitchen? What does it feel like to wake up to the ocean tides? Feel the ocean breeze coming through the windows. Remember, if you have been there in the mind, you will go there in the body, so make it happen.

7

Develop a Prosperity Mindset

You get what you think about whether you want it or not. I hope at this point those words are sinking in pretty deep. There is much wisdom in that simple little sentence. As human beings we have two choices, we can either live our lives similar to a boat lost at sea and dependent on the winds and elements to guide us or we can be the master of our own life and take charge through our thoughts.

Some people are complete victims of circumstance. They simply observe what is going on around them, accept it, and get more of it. They make little to no effort to change or better their surroundings. They have an excuse for everything and are ready at the drop of a hat to blame anybody or anything about their life situation. Their favorite phrase is "If only...". If only they were born into a different family...If only they had better genes...If only they had more opportunity to develop talent. I could go on and on, but I think you get the idea. If you are one of those people, it is time to drop your excuses, let go of the pain, take 100% responsibility for your life, and develop a prosperity consciousness.

From day one, we are bombarded with lack programming whether it is in relation to money, resources, opportunity or love. We are constantly given the message that there isn't enough to go around. We are told we live in a world of scarcity, so grab what you can, hoard it, and constantly worry about losing it. Not only have we been told that there isn't enough, but we have also been told that it is noble to be poor and that money is evil. Have you ever really thought about the idea that it is noble to be poor? So you are telling me that I should find a sense of nobility in living a life of struggle, mere survival, spiritual stagnation, and misery?

It has been said that you can't find God in a piece of bread. The reasoning behind this is that when meeting your basic needs consumes your mind, you can't think of anything else. As a result, you experience no spiritual growth whatsoever. The truth is that if you want to reach your spiritual potential, you need abundance and wealth to facilitate an environment for your soul to grow and give you the opportunity to experience life. You can't grow spiritually if you can't meet your basic needs, can't afford to buy books to read, can't experience freedom, and can't create and manifest your dreams. The purpose of life is to experience joy, expand your consciousness, and add value to the world. We are here to use our God-like ability to be creators of our experience.

Organized religions do a great job teaching and spreading lack programming. Originally the idea was to maintain power over the masses by keeping them controlled by lack programming and fear. Fear is an excellent tool of control. Being saturated with beliefs of fear and lack, individuals believe they are unworthy of abundance and that they should be satisfied with what they have. In fact, it is often taught that it is sinful to develop a desire for more. Do you see the pattern here? Lack, lack, lack, lack... It just doesn't make sense. Organized religion has the potential to taint and distort the idea of prosperity. If you choose to buy into the propaganda, you are swimming upstream and will more than likely experience difficulty obtaining prosperity in your lifetime unless you start challenging the beliefs of the masses and create your own beliefs. It is important to understand that your beliefs either work for you or against you.

I believe we are here as beings of consciousness that have been blessed with the immeasurable gift of creativity where we can use our mind and imagination to follow in the footsteps of God and create our own reality moment by moment. We are here to experience joy, abundance, love and expansion, as we take part in the wide array of diversity that complements a wide array of desires.

We are all unique beings with unique desires and dreams in which our ultimate goal is enlightenment and an expanded consciousness. Each one of us is kings and queens in our own right. Each one of us is worthy to experience the kingdom of God here on Earth.

The truth is we live in a universe of abundance. Everything that we will ever need is here with us now. Remember, everything is energy. All the energy that we will ever need already exists, perhaps just in a different form. The premise behind this fact is that there is no reason to operate from a position or mindset of lack and limitation. There is more than enough to go around. The wealth and riches that you desire already exist in the form of energy, so it is your job to convert that energy into money, a new car, or a new house.

Again, we live in a world of abundance. If someone is rich, that doesn't mean that they are taking away from the income potential of you or someone else. Money in their pocket doesn't take money out of your pocket. I often hear comments like, "How can someone spend $500 on a pair of shoes when people are homeless and starving?" This question, or something like it, always comes from a lack and limitation perspective. It is being asked from a scarcity perspective with the underlying assumption that money is finite and limited. Money is infinite and can be infinitely replenished as you reap what you sow. Because money is an infinite resource that is manifested by you, you have the control and power to make money, spend it, make more of it, and give some of it away. There is no reason to feel guilty for spoiling yourself. We are often taught that it is necessary and noble to sacrifice ourselves for the greater good of society. Again, I have to ask you, how much do you value yourself? It isn't necessary to take one for the team so to speak. When you help yourself, inevitably you are helping the whole. In fact, if you really want to help the world, it is absolutely necessary to help yourself. You will come to know that because you have the power to manifest and create more and more money, you can buy as many pairs of $500 shoes as you want, travel all around the world, drive an expensive car, and still have plenty of money left over to give to charitable causes.

So the question is - how do you go from a scarcity mindset to a prosperity consciousness? Well, it starts with your thoughts. Operating under the basic premise that you get what you think about whether you want it or not, it is important to get control of your thoughts and focus your attention on prosperity and wealth. As mentioned previously, if you focus on the lack in your life and all around you, that is exactly what you will continue to get. Your current results are a direct reflection of your past thoughts. The past doesn't have to predict the future. Change your thoughts.

Focus your attention on what you want. A really easy way to do this is to create what has been called a vision board. Get a poster board, use a wall in your bedroom, or get a corkboard, and cut out pictures of things that you want or best represent things that you want and make a montage. If you want a new Mercedes-Benz, put a picture of it on your vision board. If you want a house on the beach, find a picture of one that you like and include it. If you want a happy and fulfilling relationship, find pictures that best represent characteristics that you are looking for in a person.

By creating a vision board that you see many times during the day, you are doing a few things. For starters, you are inviting those things into your reality and sending the message to your subconscious mind that you are worthy and ready to have these things in your life. As a result, your subconscious mind will begin to pull resources within your mind and get you thinking about how you can bring this object into your reality. Remember, everything that exists in the physical world must first exist in thought form.

Also, creating a vision board helps keep your attention on what you want and it reminds you to keep your attention off of the lack that surrounds you. Keeping your attention off of the lack in your life may be difficult at first. It will take a lot of conscious effort. Every time you have a thought that is focused on the lack in your life, you must replace it with a different thought focused on prosperity and abundance. For example, when you get in your beat-down worn out car every morning, instead of focusing your thoughts on how crappy it is to drive this to work, think about the good things about it and feel grateful for it. After you remind yourself of all the good things about having a car you can drive to work, use your imagination and think about how awesome it will be to walk out to your new Mercedes-Benz and picture it in your mind. As you are driving your current car, imagine yourself driving your Mercedes-Benz. This will take practice, but over time you will cultivate your imagination and use it often. Again, focus on the good, appreciate it, and use your imagination to put yourself in the car you want. If you have been there in the mind, you will go there in the body.

As you continue to develop a prosperity mindset, it is extremely important that you don't affirm lack in your life, whether it be verbally or mentally. This can be difficult when you are surrounded by people that constantly talk about the lack in their lives. Now that you are expanding your awareness in regards to scarcity and prosperity, you will be surprised by how much lack programming surrounds you. Pay attention to your environment, pay attention to the television and the shows you watch, and pay attention to what your friends and co-workers talk about. I guarantee you will notice many more comments rooted in lack than prosperity. You will also notice that people programmed with lack obsess about money the most. They constantly talk about how they don't have enough of it, they worry about it, and they obsess about how much things cost. They live in a scarcity mindset that unfortunately will keep them there. When it comes down to it, everything revolves around scarcity in their minds. Don't be one of these people.

As you make more conscious effort to change your thoughts, you must take a good look at your beliefs around money and people with money. Unless you grew up in a vacuum, you probably have some self-limiting beliefs about money and prosperity. Perhaps, you don't believe you are worthy. Maybe you hold the belief that rich people cheated their way to the top, got lucky, or didn't have to work for it. Whatever your beliefs might be, make sure they are working for you and not against you. Your beliefs are simply thoughts that have been repeated over and over. As you change your thoughts, your beliefs will change as well.

In summary, when it comes to prosperity, you reap what you sow. The universe operates on a value exchange. As you clean up your thoughts and beliefs and start operating from a prosperity mindset, you will activate your subconscious mind and creative intellect to provide new ideas and inspired action to create the wealth that you are constantly envisioning. If you want to make more money, you must provide more value to the world. Think on that and ask yourself, "How can I provide more value to the world?" As you provide more value, the universe has no choice but to reward you with wealth.

8

Meditation

Meditation is the practice of quieting your mind and focusing your attention on one thing or nothing. It is the process of turning off the static, or habitual thought patterns, that is constantly going on in your mind. Meditation facilitates the opportunity to learn how to control your thoughts and attention. As I have mentioned, your thoughts create your world, so meditation is a great tool you can use to learn how to better control your thoughts and get a grip on the negative thought processes that are holding you back from success.

Meditation not only helps build your ability to focus, it adds stillness and serenity to your life. In your everyday life, you are bombarded with stimulation, whether it be at work, home, or school. You turn on the internet and immediately you have sources of information that are vibrationally demanding your attention. Advertisements are blinking at you, certain links are in bold, pictures with news blurbs are appearing like a slide show. You go into stimulation overload.

You get in your car and blare music or you walk into a store and they have music playing. Your cell phone has internet capability, texting, games, etc. People just don't sit still. It feels like there constantly needs to be some form of static going on in order for people to feel comfortable. Have you ever spent time with someone who can't stand silence and they feel like they need to keep talking because it is too awkward to sit in silence? Perhaps you are one of those people. These individuals also find it difficult to spend time alone not doing much of anything. Without the static, they simply don't know how to handle it. It feels very uncomfortable.

In order for you to fully reach your potential and tap into your unlimited supply of creativity, abundance, and health, you have to be able to turn off the static and listen to the silence. If there is constant static, you are cutting off your source of intuition, creativity, and inner peace. Meditation is the perfect tool to keep that gateway open.

There are many benefits of meditation that have been extensively documented in various sources. It has been estimated that twenty minutes of meditation is equivalent to two hours of sleep. Wow, talk about a trade-off!

All you would have to do is wake up 20 minutes earlier than you normally do and meditate, and not only would you be feeling more refreshed, but you would be increasing your ability to focus, be creative, and feel your intuition.

By its very nature, meditation also lowers stress levels and keeps your body healthier. Our mind, specifically our subconscious mind, manifests itself in our body. If you experience chronic physical ailments or symptoms that doctors just don't quite have answers for, more than likely, there are some negative beliefs and thought patterns that are hiding in your subconscious mind. Meditation provides an environment for you to begin the healing process and clean up your conscious and subconscious mind. Get started because until you rid your mind of self-limiting and negative beliefs, you will not get the results you want.

Alright, you might be asking yourself," Okay, how do I get started?" The first thing you will want to do is pick a quiet place in your home where you will be completely free from interruption. Do not pick your bed. Beds are for sleeping, so if you try to meditate in bed, more than likely you will fall asleep because your body has been trained to sleep in bed. Pick a different location whether it is the couch in your office, a chair in the den, or the lawn chair in the backyard. The important thing is that it is a spot where you are free from any interruption. With practice you will be able to put yourself in a meditative state anywhere, but for starters it is important to begin here.

Once you pick your location, set aside at least 15-30 minutes. If you prefer, you can set an alarm to manage the time. It might be good to start with 15 minutes and as you get more capable, you can extend it to 30 minutes or more. So get comfortable, close your eyes, and try to relax your entire body. Try to feel your energy in your body. An easy way to focus and eliminate the static of other random thoughts in your mind is to focus on your breathing and with every breath count backwards from 25. As you focus on your breathing, breathing in and out, visualize the oxygen being transferred from your lungs to your blood vessels and try to feel the healing and nourishing power that is traveling through your body. With each breath, count backwards from 25 not allowing any other thoughts to enter your mind. Focus 100% on your breathing. If random thoughts enter your mind, acknowledge them and let them go as you breathe out. Ideally, after 25 breaths you will find yourself in a relaxed meditative state where you can continue to focus on your breathing or use various visualization techniques to keep your mind focused.

In James Arthur Ray's book, *Harmonic Wealth*, he talks about four categories of meditation including The Focusing/Visualization Mediation, Listening of Watching, Static Transcendence, and Mobile Transcendence. The Focusing/Visualization Meditation is a great place to start and to gain some experience meditating.

There are six different Focusing/Visualization Meditations that James Arthur Ray introduces that I would like to share with you. The first is called the Candle Meditation. While doing this meditation, sit in a dark room while staring at a candle flame. Your goal is to become the flame so to speak. When your thoughts wander in any type of direction, you must direct your thoughts back to the flame. This process trains your mind to focus and move in one controlled direction.

Another type of meditation is called Cloud Play. This meditation is done with your eyes open. Lie on your back in your yard or at the park. Now, with your mind, punch holes in the clouds. Visualize a hole in the cloud and do it intensely. You will notice that the hole actually appears. If you don't believe me, try it!

Guided Meditation is another type of meditation where you simply use a mediation CD. There are many to choose from at your local bookstore. The purpose behind guided meditations is that they keep your conscious mind entertained by giving it something to listen to while training it to focus in a certain direction.

Another example from this category of meditation is the Grandfather Clock Meditation. During this meditation, you sit with your eyes closed and visualize a grandfather clock in full detail including the wood finish, the swinging pendulum, and all of the sounds. You want to clearly see it in your mind's eye. You can actually do this with any object that you want to create in your life including a new car, house, pair of shoes, etc. The important thing is that you use all of your sensory factors while visualizing and make sure you can hear it, see it, smell it, and feel it.

Another visualization technique that James talks about is choosing one train of thought and following it without letting anything else come into your mind. For example, if you want to write a book, with your eyes closed, think about the process from beginning to end of writing that book. Visualize yourself gathering research, picking a title, putting together an outline, writing the pages, finding a publisher, and then finally selling the book. A few things to keep in mind while doing this include keeping it in the present tense and always bringing it to a positive conclusion while keeping negative thoughts out of the picture.

As you can see, there are many different techniques that you can use to train your mind to focus through meditation. Personally, meditation has been life changing for me. I used to be one of those people who had to be constantly going. I was anxious a lot of the time, felt hurried, felt a lot of internal and external pressure because of expectations, worried a lot, had a hard time sleeping, etc. I was lost in the static and looking back it was as if I were a dog constantly chasing my tail and getting nowhere. I lacked focus, and I lacked peace. I had completely shut off my ability to feel me and my energy. I eventually learned there was no amount of action that I could do to overcompensate for the fact that I had cut off my supply to my creative source and intuition.

As I began meditating, I experienced a complete shift in consciousness. As I would focus on my breathing, it brought me to the present. I no longer needed anxiety and worry to function. I felt more power without them, and I still do. As I have increased my personal power, I have also increased my inner peace. I officially made it out of the static. Phew!

Not only did meditation help get my mind in the present, but it continues to teach me how to focus and control my mind. Until you control your mind, you are at the mercy of the wind and of your internal programming. The question that you need to ask yourself is this," Are you doing the thinking or are you being thought?" Until you focus your mind and consciously choose your thoughts, you are being thought. Take control of who you are and where you are going and use meditation as a tool to help you get there.

9

Read Two Books a Month

Growing up, I remember it feeling like a complete chore to read a book. In school, I remember being assigned so many books to read for English class and feeling a complete sense of obligation to read the books. There wasn't much enjoyment involved, but I would do it anyway and as necessary would employ my skim-reading techniques to speed up the process. I imagine I missed out on some great material as I sped through books with the only intention of passing a test or writing a paper.

It wasn't until after I graduated high school that my love for reading took off. Perhaps it was because I wasn't obligated to read a book that someone else picked and have it read by a certain date and time. I was on my own schedule, and I was in control, and to top that off, I wanted answers. I was at a point in my life where the paradigm that I was forced to adopt as a small child no longer applied or coincided with my view of the world, and it was time for me to find my truth and find my answers. I needed answers that the people in my life couldn't give me because I wanted to aspire to a place that they had never been.

So the journey began with one small step at a time. Page by page, I developed a stronger sense of myself, the world, and what it all means to me. In addition to enrolling in college and eventually receiving a Master's degree, I made it a priority to continue reading on my own. I found myself constantly intrigued with books in the self-improvement section because I felt I had broken or missing pieces in my soul that only I had the power to fix. I then moseyed my way over to the business section and dabbled a bit there. I wanted to read and learn from people who had cultivated the level of success that I wanted so badly to experience for myself. I figured they must be doing something right, and I had much to learn.

Over time, I made my way from book to book expanding my knowledge and understanding of the human spirit, myself, and gaining a better understanding of what it means to be truly happy. It is funny because I went from a kid who read books out of complete obligation and disgruntlement to someone who can't seem to read enough. Books are one of the many jewels of this earth and learning is a critical piece of expansion and self-improvement.

It has often been said that leaders are readers, and quite honestly, I think it is safe to say that there are no exceptions to that. If you want to become "bigger" than you are and achieve better results, you have to become an expert in your own right. You can't do that without reading and gaining the knowledge necessary to achieve your goals and dreams. Remember, the key here is that you have to become "bigger" than you are to get better results. You can't become bigger than you are by plopping yourself on the sofa and putting yourself in a self-induced coma as you watch television for hours at a time.

With that said, to give yourself a nice push in the direction of your dreams, it would be a good idea to make the goal of reading at least two books a month. If that feels like a lot, then start with one book a month, but two books is definitely manageable. How bad do you want a better life? If you value it, you will make the time.

Now you might be asking yourself," Well, I don't even know where to start…What books should I be reading?" You could really go in a couple directions. If you know exactly what you want to do, then start reading books about people who have succeeded in those areas. Read books that tell their story and give insight into how they were able to be successful. Start reading books that educate you on your desired profession. Saturate yourself with knowledge. This would allow you to slowly become an expert in your field and give you a huge edge over the competition. If you are unsure about what you want to do but you know that no matter what you want to be success-ful, read books about what it takes to be successful. This book is a perfect example of that. Read others as well. Read books that talk about wealth and how to attain it.

There is so much information available within your grasp. If you are at a place in your life where you can't afford to buy books, take advantage of the library or simply hang out at the bookstore and read for an hour a day. Just do it. Similar to what happened to me, you will get sucked into it, and you will find yourself making it a priority to read every day regardless of other things that are going on in your life.

Remember, success just doesn't drop in your lap. You have to work for it and put yourself in vibrational alignment with it. What you want wants you. Reading two books a month will accelerate your path to success, give you an edge above your competition, and keep you in a learning mindset. Learning should never stop. The more you learn, the more you know. The more you know, the more value you can give to the world. The more value that you can give to the world, the more money you will make. Always remember that. If you want to make more money, you should be constantly asking yourself, "How can I provide more value to the world?"

Increase the value that you can provide to the world by educating yourself and learning new things through books. A person who doesn't read is no more effective than a person who can't read. Make the time and read some books.

10

Focus on Your Success

At this point, you should be fairly familiar with the universal Law of Attraction and the importance of paying attention to your thoughts and beliefs. Our beliefs and thoughts fuel and determine our feelings and behavior. Our behavior then creates our habits, which in turn creates our reality. Based on evidence of this universal law, it completely makes no sense to put your energy and attention on things that you don't want - not even for a second. Focus on what you do want because ultimately what you think about it is what you get.

The fact is energy flows where attention goes, and your thoughts manifest themselves in your reality. Because this is the case, it is important to focus on your successes instead of focusing on your failures. As you set your sights on what you want, your goal is to create a success mindset that you habitually operate.

Every memory and the essence of every experience are stored in your nervous system including your feelings, thoughts, and interpretations. Your brain uses these memories to form your beliefs about yourself and the world around you and then uses those beliefs to mold your habits and reactionary thought patterns.

For example, if throughout your life you dwelled on your failures and allowed yourself to feel like a failure, your nervous system stores this mode of operation and creates a habit and thought pattern that creates more failure. Failure becomes your reactionary method of operation until you consciously make the effort to change it.

Keep in mind, your brain and nervous system can't tell the difference between a real experience or an imagined experience. When a goal is set or you have a goal in mind and you use your imagination to visualize it and evoke feelings of having accomplished the goal, your nervous system and brain stores this information and activates your internal servo-mechanism to make it happen. The key here is to use your imagination to bring your dreams, ideas, and thoughts to the physical realm.

Something that is important to understand is that this can work positively for you as well as negatively. For example, on the positive side, you could have a goal in mind, visualize and think about it, and evoke feelings of self-confidence, contentment, and success. On the other hand, you could have a goal in mind, visualize and think about it, and evoke feelings of anxiety, worry, inadequacy, and failure.

In either case, your nervous system and brain over time not only creates a reactionary and habitual mode of operation based on your thoughts and feelings, but your thoughts and feelings become a determining factor of your results. The important thing to keep in mind is that you get what you focus your thoughts and energy on whether you want it or not.

So my question for you is this, how often do you feel anxious, worrisome, or inadequate? Your answer to this question should give you a good idea as to how much of your energy is focused on the possibility of failure rather than the possibility of success regardless of the situation or circumstances.

If you want to create and experience success in your life consistently, it is necessary to form a reactionary and habitual mode of operation where you expect success every time and you automatically evoke the feeling of success. In order to create this habit, there are a few things you can do. First, pay attention to your thoughts and feelings when you have a goal or task in mind. Visualize yourself accomplishing the goal or task with ease and focus on what you can control. Try to evoke feelings associated with the accomplishment. While you visualize, try to evoke the same feelings that would be present if you already accomplished it. Ask yourself, "How would

I feel if I achieved this?" Picture it. Feel it. Focus all of your thoughts and energy on a successful outcome.

Second, throughout the day, point out your successes to yourself, whether they be large or small. Immediately after you accomplish a task or goal throughout the day, acknowledge it. Tell yourself that you did an excellent job, evoke the feeling of success, and allow the nurturing of your self-confidence.

The end of the day is a great time to acknowledge your successes. Right before you go to sleep, think about your victories for the day and remind yourself how good it felt to accomplish those tasks and goals. For those days that you have a hard time thinking of any successes during the day, relive and think about successes from the past and try to evoke those feelings associated with accomplishment. The important thing here is to focus your attention on your successes and create a habit out of feeling successful.

This creates the habit of focusing your attention on what you want. I think it is safe to assume you want success and you want to build on the success you have already had. The fact is success breeds success. When you are operating from a success mindset, you set yourself up for more success. It is that simple.

Conclusion

Success is well within your reach. Now that your mind has been opened to the universal truths shared in this book, you are closer than you have ever been. Gain control of your thoughts, take responsibility for your life, act more from your desired outcome, utilize the indisputable laws of the universe, cultivate your mind, and develop a prosperity and success mindset. You are on your way to turning the tide in your life and finally making your way to happiness, joy, success, peace, and fulfillment.

Maintain this momentum and feed your mind with other great books related to the concepts discussed here. If you are unsure of what books to read, a great place to start is the bibliography following this conclusion. Begin to cultivate the garden in your mind with these powerful ideas as you apply them in your life.

Remember, success doesn't drop in your lap. You have to work for it and put yourself in vibrational alignment with it. What you want wants you. As you project the desire for success into your future, it is up to you to "catch up" to it through your thoughts, feelings, and actions.

Life is about growth, expansion, and joy. Make the decision to become the person you would need to be in order to experience the level of success you want. Grow bigger and act from the outcome. The time is now to turn the tide in your life and move in the direction of your dreams. Make decisions based on where you are going not where you have been, and always keep in mind that your past results will not dictate your future outcomes if you take responsibility and change your thoughts.

Your past results are nothing more than a direct reflection of your past thoughts. Change your thoughts, and you will automatically change your results. Think, visualize, and feel your way to your success. It is patiently waiting for you, so you better get on your way…one thought at a time.

Thank you so much for taking the time to read this book. I truly appreciate it. As you live your life, you have two choices in regards to time. You can spend it or invest it. Reading this book was an excellent investment as it has opened your mind and heart to your infinite power and capability. My heart rests in appreciation, excitement, and peace knowing you are on your way to your dreams. Having been there myself, I can attest to the fact that it is a wonderful feeling. Enjoy the ride.

Bibliography

Allen, James. *Selected Teachings of James Allen*. Virginia: Wilder Publications, 2007.

Canfield, Jack. *The Success Principles – How to Get from Where You Are to Where You Want to Be*. New York: HarperCollins, 2007.

Gage, Randy. *Prosperity Mind – How to Harness the Power of Thought*. Kansas: Prime Concepts Publishing, 2003.

Hicks, Esther and Jerry. *The Law of Attraction*. California: Hay House, 2006.

Hill, Napoleon. *Think & Grow Rich*. New York: Random House, 1983.

Maltz, Maxwell. *Psycho-Cybernetics*. New York: Pocket Books, 1960.

Murphy, Dr. Joseph. *The Power of Your Subconscious Mind*. New York: Reward Books, 2000.

Ray, James A. *Harmonic Wealth – The Secret of Attracting the Life You Want*. New York: Hyperion, 2008.

Ray, James A. *The Science of Success*. California: Sunark Press, 2006.

www.ingramcontent.com/pod-product-compliance
Lightning Source LLC
Chambersburg PA
CBHW071623040426
42452CB00009B/1452